250 Random
Shoula Know

A collection of random facts useful for the odd pub quiz night get-together or as conversation starters.

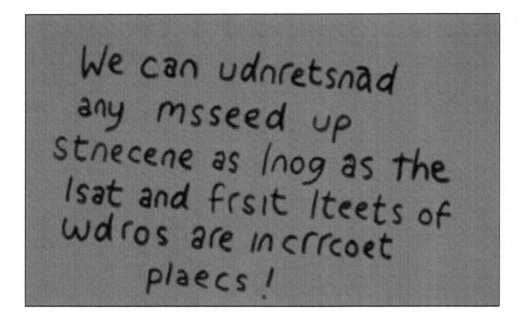

We can udnretsnad any msseed up stnecene as lnog as the lsat and frsit lteets of wdros are incrrcoet plaecs!

Have you ever had that moment when you are in the middle of a conversation and suddenly the room becomes quiet and nobody knows how to move the discussion forward?

Have you ever wondered why people can effortlessly drive conversations by dropping quirky and weird tidbits here and there to keep people interested and engaged?

Have you ever had moments when you wish you knew something that others don't, so you can catch their attention and command the room?

Of course, you do. Haven't we all?

It's for this reason that we decided to write this book.

You never know when some of these facts can come in handy as a conversation starter or something that you can use to move the conversation along. You never know when you can use these facts to pick up girls, or for girls to one-up men who think they know everything.

Besides, it's just plain fun reading about these quirky and weird facts that range from funny to downright surprising.

Whatever your motivation is, there's a really good chance that you'll find these facts and tidbits useful; or, it's also possible that you'll find these facts useless, but then again, isn't that what the internet is for?

So if you're ready, here are 250 facts that everyone should know about!

250 Random Facts Everyone Should Know

Dig in!

All about Animals

Image credit: www.chicahood.com

1. A crocodile cannot stick out its tongue.

2. A shrimp's heart is in its head.

3. Pigs cannot look up into the sky. Because of their very short necks, their range of motion is limited that they cannot look up at the sky from a normal standing position.

4. It's a common misconception that ostriches bury their heads in the sand when they are afraid. They wouldn't be able to breathe if they did this. A study of 200,000 ostriches conducted over an 80-year period (yes, some people were that determined!) claimed that there has not been a reported instance where an ostrich buried its head in the sand. (Bonus fact: Ostriches run faster than horses and the males can roar like lions. If it was up to me, there is no reason for an ostrich to

stand still and hide its head when it can simply run away from the thing that's scaring it!)

5. Rats and horses cannot vomit. But we don't need to know any more about that, do we?

6. Rats are so adept at reproduction that if you started with 2 rats, there would be more than a million descendants after an 18-month period.

7. A duck's quack doesn't echo. At least that's what people have come to believe. The next time you hear someone say that, tell them they're wrong. Duck quacks do echo!

8. A crocodile cannot chew. It also cannot move its tongue. And as if that's not enough, its digestive juices are so strong that they can digest a steel nail in just a few days.

9. Camels are called "ships of the desert" but that is not because they transport cargo over huge distances. Instead, it's because of the way they move. The humps in a camel look like waves so as the camel moves, its head appears to be moving against the backdrop of its wavy humps. The humps are also used as fat storage so if your camel is undernourished, it will not have a hump.

10. A sloth's digestion is, well, sloth-like. It is so slow that it actually takes two weeks for a sloth to digest its food.

11. Experiments have shown that male rhesus macaque monkeys will "pay" for them to look at pictures of female rhesus

macaques' bottoms. Apparently, someone thought this was a worthwhile academic venture.

12. Rabbits and guinea pigs cannot sweat. Both animals have no sweat glands.

13. There are only two animals known to man that don't get cancer. These are rays and sharks. Let's hope that scientists can figure out why and put it to good use.

14. There's still some debate as to whether or not dolphins or porpoises are the second most intelligent animal on the planet. (Let's suppose, for the sake of argument, that man is the first, although there's still some debate about that as well). Both animals are known to recognize their own reflections and have been characterized as having the intelligence equivalent to that of a second-grader.

15. Beavers take care of their young for up to two years before they are made to leave the nest.

16. Skunks are sharpshooters. They can accurately spray their smelly fluid as far away as ten feet. They prefer to blast away with no regard for what's in their path. However, if necessary, they can be accurate shooters too.

17. Deer can't eat hay.

18. In Arizona, gopher snakes are not poisonous. However, they do a pretty good imitation of rattlesnakes by hissing and shaking their tails when frightened.

19. It is common fact that dogs have a much better sense of smell than humans. However, dogs also have better eyesight, on average. The caveat is that dogs only see in a narrow range of colors so their world is certainly not as colorful.

20. The duckbill platypus stores worms in the pouches of its cheeks, sometimes as many as six hundred at any one time. What it does with this, I do not want to know and you shouldn't bother asking either.

21. North American oysters do not make pearls of any value. These oysters are great for eating but for your pearly needs, you have to turn to something else.

22. Hammerhead sharks give birth to live young, which is surprising for a couple of reasons. First, most sharks lay eggs instead of giving birth. Second, have you seen a hammerhead shark? I mean, of all the sharks in the world, hammerheads are the least preferable for live birth because of the shape of their heads. Thankfully, they manage by folding their hammer-shaped heads back and that takes care of that.

23. Gorillas spend up to 14 hours a day sleeping.

24. Golden toads are becoming so rare that a biological preserve has been made to protect them.

25. Kangaroos all look the same, don't they? Well, the truth is that there are more than fifty different types of kangaroos.

26. Most types of jellyfish prefer salt water to fresh water.

27. Female lions in a pride perform ninety percent of the hunting. When the catch is made, male lions – particularly the dominant ones in the pride – come in to eat the "lionshare" of the serving. How's that for laziness?

28. A man in Boulder Junction, Wisconsin, once took a picture of three albino deer in the woods near his house. This wouldn't have been a big deal except for the fact that the odds of finding three albino deer in one location is one in seventy nine billion. Take that, lotto gods.

29. We've also referred to any group of cows as a herd but the official term for a group of twelve or more cows is a "flink."

30. When cats rub against your leg or against furniture, they are simply marking their territory. Cats usually rub their faces because this is where their scent glands are located.

31. Cats sleep up to eighteen hours in a day. They never fall too deeply asleep because they always wake up to check if their surroundings are still safe. The next time that you see your cat lounging around, you can bet they're sleeping; not as deeply as would want to if it was you, but they are certainly sleeping.

32. Catnip is an herb which contains nepetalactone which is believed to make cats "high."

33. Most male horses have 40 teeth while females only have 36. You can use this to tell the sex of a horse assuming that you can get into a horse's mouth.

34. If catnips can make a cat high, you can use a tiny amount of liquor to provide the same effect on a scorpion. Drop it in a tiny amount of liquor and it will go mad and, in certain cases, sting itself to death.

35. Ever wonder how orcas, or killer whales, kill sharks? They torpedo from the bottom of the seafloor into the shark's stomach. If done correctly, this can cause a shark to explode.

36. Not everything exotic "tastes like chicken." Beetles are said to taste like apples, wasps like pine nuts, and worms like fried bacon. We can't personally verify this fact but we doubt you'd care.

37. A cockroach won't die from having its head severed. If you cut off its head, it can continue to live for several weeks. It will only eventually die because of starvation.

38. The elephant is the only mammal that can't jump! This is probably why jump ropes for elephants have not yet been invented.

39. Camels are specifically evolved to be comfortable in the desert. One adaption is that they have three eyelids to protect themselves from the blowing sand.

40. Do you ever doubt the sure-footedness of a donkey? According to biologists, the placement of a donkey's eyes allows it to see all four feet at all times!

41. Dolphins sleep with one eye open! This allows them to rest half of their brain at any one time. After a few minutes, they switch to the other eye to rest the other part of their brain.

42. Slugs have 4 noses.

43. Most birds cannot see the color blue. Owls are the only exception to this fact.

44. A giraffe's tongue is so long and dexterous that it can be used to clean its ears.

45. An ostrich's eye is about the same size as its brain. You can't fault an ostrich for not being smart but those guns it calls legs more than make up for the lack in smarts.

46. A pig's orgasm lasts 30 minutes. Lucky duck!

47. For the male praying mantis, sex is the ultimate sacrifice. The female initiates sex by ripping the male's head off which causes the male mantis' body to contort so it can copulate with the female. See, the pig is really one lucky duck.

48. The taste sensors of butterflies are located at the bottom of their feet. Literally, they taste with their feet.

49. A cat's urine glows under a UV light. There are other bodily effusions that glow under a UV light but of course you already know that.

50. Polar bears are left-handed.

51. Humans and dolphins are the only species that have sex for pleasure. But then again, pig orgasms last 30 minutes so there's that.

52. The silkworm is so gluttonous that it consumes 86,000 times its own weight in 56 days.

53. A dog's mouth is just as dirty – if not dirtier – than a human's.

54. The western spotted skunk is one of a handful of animals that can delay their pregnancy for up to a few months. No word yet on the reasons why skunks will opt for this child-bearing strategy.

55. Pink flamingos are not born pink. They eventually get their color from the pigments in the food they eat.

56. Female kangaroos have three vaginas.

57. The loneliest creature on Earth is a whale who calls on a different frequency so other whales cannot hear him. As a result, he has been calling out for a mate for over two decades to no avail. Scientists have tracked his movements globally over that period. (There's also no word on how lonely these scientists are for spending their lives tracking a lonely whale.)

58. The northern leopard frog swallows its prey using its eyes. To help push food down its throat, the toad has to retract its eyes into its head. Seriously, you can't make this up.

59. There is a single mega-colony of ants that is situated on three continents. The colony covers much of Europe, as far as the

west coast of the U.S. to the west, and the west coast of Japan to the east.

60. The biggest organism known today is a fungus which occupies a combined area of 2.4 miles in the Blue Mountains of Oregon. The fungus is connected by an intricate network of root systems and all parts of the fungi are genetically identical.

All about the Human Body

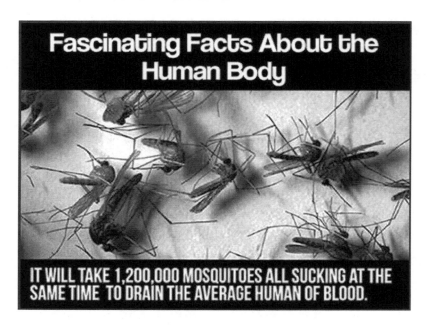

Image credit: www.funporo.com

61. When you sneeze, people say "bless you" because your heart literally stops for a millisecond. That might not seem like much but consider the consequences if it doesn't restart after that momentary stop? Yeah, bless you.

62. Don't try to suppress a sneeze. If you do, there's a good chance you can rupture a blood vessel in your head or neck. There's also a good chance you can fracture a rib if you sneeze too hard.

63. If you try and keep your eyes open when you sneeze, you might pop out an eyeball. Thankfully, it's impossible to keep your eyes open, without any external intervention, otherwise the consequences can be deadly.

64. It is NOT impossible to lick your elbow. It's just that not everyone can do it. In addition, over 75% of people who read this for the first time will try to lick their elbow.

65. Like fingerprints, everyone's tongue print is different. And so are your eyes, which is why it's now being used in retinal scans. We're only waiting for the tongue scanners to start rolling in and then we're set.

66. You can live without food for about a month. However, you can only live about a week without water. Your body automatically triggers you to feel thirsty if the amount of water in your body is reduced by 1%. If it's reduced by 10%, however, there's a good chance you'll die.

67. An aspirin can indeed save your life during a heart attack but you have to be able to chew it for it to work.

68. Every year about 98% of the atoms in your body are replaced. That's astounding considering that the average adult is made up of 7,000,000,000,000,000,000,000,000,000 individual atoms.

69. We all spent about half an hour as a single cell. That's astounding.

70. The stomach produces a new layer of mucus every two weeks. If it fails to do so, it will end up digesting itself.

71. You can't kill yourself by holding your breath. Seriously, stop trying.

72. One quarter of the bones in your body are in your feet!

73. Most dust particles in your house are made from dead skin! Individually, our body sheds about 600,000 particles of skin every hour.

74. Women blink nearly twice as much as men. No one knows why.

75. A baby has about 90 more bones than an adult. Many of the bones fuse together as we grow older.

76. A man named Charles Osborne had the hiccups for 69 years!

77. The human heart is so powerful that it creates enough pressure to squirt blood 30 feet when it pumps.

78. There are about 60,000 miles of blood vessels in the human body. If you laid them end to end, they would stretch around the world more than twice.

79. The longest time between two twins being born is 87 days.

80. An average person produces about 25,000 quarts of saliva in a lifetime. That's enough to fill two swimming pools. Finding

somebody willing to swim in those pools is something else entirely.

81. The human body contains enough iron to make one 3-inch iron nail.

82. Your sweat is odorless, and so is mine! That stinky smell you're sniffing doesn't come from the sweat but from the bacteria that feeds on the sweat.

83. When awake, the human brain produces enough electricity to power a small light bulb. And you think the machines in The Matrix were crazy, huh?

84. Along the same lines, the human heart creates enough energy in a day's work to drive a truck 20 miles.

85. While awake, we spend about 10% of the time with our eyes closed because we're blinking.

86. The human eye's resolution is equivalent to a 576-megapixel camera. Even the best camera manufacturers in the world still have a ways to go before producing a camera that can equal the capacity of the human eye.

87. When combined and weighed separately, all the bacteria in the body of an average adult will be equal to about 4 pounds.

88. Your brain is a relatively small part of your body but it uses 20% of the oxygen and blood.

89. Human bones are hard. Pound-for-pound, they are stronger than steel. But they are also made up of 31% water.

90. Your DNA is locked up in the nucleus of your cells, tightly coiled in a helix structure. If uncoiled and joined end-to-end, all the DNA in your body would stretch 10 billion miles, about the same distance from the Earth to Pluto and back.

All about the World's Different Cultures and Customs

Image credit: www.techwomen.org

91. We all think cell phones are now ubiquitous. However, more than 50% of the people in the world have never made or received a telephone call.

92. According to a study conducted by the Economic Research Service, about 27% of all food production in Western nations

ends up in garbage cans. Ironically, it is estimated that about 1.2 billion people worldwide are underfed.

93. Fun fact: what is called a "French kiss" in the English-speaking world is known as an "English kiss" in France.

94. In Iceland, it's against the law to have a pet dog.

95. In Nebraska in the US, it's against the law to sneeze, or burp, in a church.

96. The names of Native American children were typically taken from the first thing that their parents saw when they left their tepees at the time of the child's birth. This led to names such as Sitting Bull and Running Water. Thus far, however, we do not know of anyone named Crapping Bull or Stinky Water so there must be some luck involved in the process.

97. The Matami Tribe of West Africa play their own version of football. In place of the normal football, they use a human skull.

98. Travelling masseuses in ancient Japan were required by law to be blind. Nobody knows why.

99. The "Freedom of Speech" provision in the First Amendment protects you from punishment from the government. However, this does not exempt you from the potential consequences of your speech. This is why you can be sued for libel, or punched on the street for talking too much.

100. Before 1920, it was illegal for women in the United States to vote. Women rights advocate Susan B. Anthony tried to vote in 1872. As punishment, she was arrested and fined $100.

101. There is a town in the United States where it is illegal for chickens to cross the road. The town's name is Quitman, Georgia.

102. In Michigan, it is illegal for residents to tie a crocodile onto a fire hydrant. Yes, that's a law.

103. In the state of Louisiana in the United States, you can get fined $500 if you ask a pizza delivery guy to deliver pizza to a friend without him knowing ahead of time.

104. This is not a custom but if you have $10 in the United States and you don't owe anybody anything, you are wealthier than 25% of all Americans.

105. In the US alone, exposure to second-hand smoke is responsible for about 50,000 deaths per year.

All about Everyday Products

Image credit: www.cracked.com

106. In the course of an average lifetime you will, while sleeping, eat 70 assorted insects and 10 spiders. Enjoy.

107. Here's a sure-fire way to increase the bacteria in your ears: wear headphones. Just an hour spent using headphones increases the bacteria in your ear by about 700 times.

108. Most types of lipstick contain fish scales.

109. On average, about 50% of all false teeth contain some form of radioactivity.

110. Starch is the substance used as a binder in paper. The amount of starch used controls the level of ink penetration when printing. Cheaper papers scrimp on starch. This is why you get that black residue on your elbows when you lean over your morning paper.

111. Sterling silver is not made of pure silver. It consists of 92.5% silver and 7.5% copper. The addition of copper is necessary

because pure silver is too soft and won't be of much use as tableware or coins.

112. The wick of a trick candle has small amounts of magnesium in it. When the flame is blown out, the magnesium inside the wick doesn't go out. After a few seconds, it re-lights the wick, hence the "trick."

113. The Heinz ketchup bottle used to be marketed with that iconic "57". This represented the 57 different varieties of pickles that the company once had.

114. Here's one for all of you science geeks: When you drop a raisin into a glass of fresh champagne, it will bob up and down continuously.

115. In the 1830s, ketchup was sold as medicine. And so was Coca-Cola.

116. If you want to lose weight, try incorporating celery into your diet. It takes more calories to eat a piece of celery than what the celery can provide. The same is true of apples.

117. Do you cry when you peel and chop onions? Try chewing gum!

118. Just in case you're wondering, the glue used on Israeli postage stamps is certified kosher.

119. Honey is the only food that does not spoil. That's just fine considering that to produce a single pound of honey, a single bee would have to visit 2 million flowers.

120. Coca-Cola would be green if coloring weren't added to it.

121. The FDA permits up to 5 whole insects per 100 grams of apple butter. However, it doesn't say that the insects really need to be "whole", only that the maximum equivalent of 5 whole insects is in the butter. I know, it's mind-boggling, right?

122. There are no naturally occurring blue foods. Nothing. Even blueberries are purple!

123. If you want your buttered toast to land butter-side up, it is recommended that you drop it from a minimum height of 8 feet.

124. Casu marzu is a Sardinian cheese that contains live maggots. Let me repeat that: live maggots! Bon appetit.

125. Pennies and nickels are money pits. They cost more to make than they're actually worth. In 2013, US taxpayers lost over $100 million just to make these coins.

All about Pop Culture

Image credit: www.challengereagles.edublogs.org

126. In every episode of Seinfeld there is a Superman somewhere.

127. The cigarette lighter was invented before the match. There are some questions as to the definition of match and lighter. However, according to historians, the first match was invented in 1826 while the first lighter came out in 1823, 3 years before the match.

128. Fun fact: Thirty-five percent of people who use personal dating ads are already married. Well, maybe it isn't fun if you happen to be the spouse of someone who just ran a personal dating ad. Yeah, moving on!

129. Fun but stupid fact: 23% of all photocopier faults worldwide are caused by people sitting on them and photocopying their butts. Okay, maybe there's some sampling error in those statistics but c'mon, how can people be so stupid as to really try photocopying their butts?

130. The Grammy Awards were first introduced to counter the threat of rock music.

131. The first fossilized specimen of *Australopithecus Afarenisis* was named Lucy because the palaeontologists who discovered the specimen were so in-love with the song "Lucy in the Sky with Diamonds" by The Beatles.

132. During the chariot scene in "Ben Hur" a small red car can be seen in the distance. Okay, maybe not! But in the movie Schindler's List – which was completely in black and white – there was a scene were a little girl wearing a red dress was clearly shown walking amongst the Nazi soldiers. Now that's great filmmaking.

133. True fact: Donald Duck comics were banned from Finland. Why? Because Donald isn't wearing any pants.

134. In the US, liquor was banned in the 1920s. This period was called "Prohibition" and the underground market was responsible for the rise of the great gangsters like Al Capone.

135. During World War II, the US almost depleted all of its metal to make weapons of war. During this time, the trophies given during the Oscars were made from wood.

136. There are no clocks in Las Vegas gambling casinos.

137. If a month begins on a Sunday, it will always have a "Friday the 13th."

138. The average person spends 2 weeks of their lives waiting for the light to change from red to green. Now, for all our sakes,

please don't ask how much time people spend sitting in their cars waiting for the traffic to move.

139. Along the same lines, the average American spends about 18 months of his or her life watching commercials on television.

140. Most Muppets are left-handed.

141. Because of the property of metals, the top of the Eiffel Tower moves as much as 7 inches during the day. This is because the metal facing the sun heats up and expands..

142. The Ms in M&Ms stand for Mars and Murrie which are the last names of the inventors of the now famous candies.

143. Beyoncé has a species of fly named in her honor. The fly, appropriately enough, is known as the "Bootylicious species."

144. Pandas are endemic to China. That means that all pandas in the world are basically Chinese.

145. The set used in the 2009 Sherlock Holmes film was eventually re-used as the set for Sirius Black's house in Harry Potter: Order of the Phoenix. Yes, even big budget movies try to save a few dollars here and there.

All about Words and Languages

146. You'd think they'd be more careful but in the 1996 edition of Webster's Dictionary, 315 words were misspelled.

147. The name Wendy was first used in the book Peter Pan. You could say that it was specifically made up for that book. There was never a recorded Wendy in history prior to the book's publication!

148. There are no words in the dictionary that rhyme with: orange and purple! So if you write poems, try to stay away from ending a line with purple or orange.

149. The word "queue" is the only word in the English language that is pronounced in the same way even if you remove the last four letters of the word.

150. The longest word in the English language with all the letters in alphabetical order? "Almost."

Of the 17k+ words used by Shakespeare, he invented about 1,700 of them including: addiction, gossip, and lackluster.

Image credit: www.wtffunfact.com

151. The longest English word without a vowel: "Rhythm".

152. The five official languages of the United Nations are: English, Arabic, Chinese, Russian and Spanish.

153. Gnurr. That's the official name used to refer to the lint that collects at the bottom of your pocket.

154. The longest village name in the world is Llanfairpwllgwyngyllgogerychwyrndrobwyll llantysiliogogogoch and it is located in Wales.

155. As of today, only two words in the English language end in – gry. These are "angry" and "hungry."

156. The words "bookkeeper" and "bookkeeping" are the only unhyphenated English word with three consecutive double letters. Other words like "sweet-toothed" already need a hyphen.

157. The word "uncopyrightable" is the longest English word in normal use that contains no letter more than once.

158. A sentence that contains all 26 letters of the alphabet is called a "pangram". The most common example is "The quick brown fox jumps over the lazy dog." This sentence is also often used to test keyboards to check that all letter keys are functioning.

159. Words that are formed by combining two words together are known as a "portmanteau." Common examples include brunch and motel.

160. The shortest complete sentence in the English language is "I am."

All about History

Former US President Calvin Coolidge (1924-28) enjoyed "buzzing for his bodyguards and then hiding under his desk as they frantically searched for him"

Image credit: www.wtffunfact.com

161. The US bills are not made from paper. The material used is a combination of cotton and linen. There was a brief period in 1932 when notes were made from wood due to the need to quickly print money during a shortage.

162. The tea bag was introduced in 1908 by Thomas Sullivan of New York. Tea, however, is said to have been discovered in 2700 BC when a Chinese emperor accidentally knocked off some tea leaves into a pot of boiling water.

163. In 1955 the richest woman in the world was Mrs. Hetty Green Wilks. She left an estate amounting to $95 million. Her will

was found stashed in a tin box together with four pieces of soap.

164. During World War II, the crew of the British submarine HMS Trident kept a fully grown reindeer called Pollyanna for six weeks. Let's just say people have done crazier things while on long ocean voyages.

165. The first projection of an image on a screen is credited to German priest Athanasius Kircher in 1646. He used an oil lamp to project hand-painted images onto a white screen. The idea was further developed by Joseph Niepce who made the first photographic image in 1827, and by Thomas Edison and W K L Dickson who introduced the film camera in 1894.

166. There have been instances where Oscar awards were refused by their respective awardees. In 1935, writer Dudley Nichols refused to accept the award because the Writers Guild was on strike. In 1970, George Scott did not accept the Best Actor Oscar for Patton while in 1972, Marlon Brando refused the Oscar for his role in The Godfather.

167. The system of democracy was developed 2,500 years ago in Athens, Greece.

168. Fun fact: the original Declaration of Independence is written on hemp paper.

169. A pig in France was once executed in public by hanging for the murder of a child. This happened in 1386.

170. Queen Elizabeth I regarded herself as an example of personal cleanliness. She declared that she bathed once every three months, whether she needed it or not.

171. Claudette Colvin was the first black woman not to give up her seat to a white woman on a bus, not Rosa Parks. This happened 9 months before the famous Rosa Parks incident.

172. In 1811 and 1812, earthquakes registering 8 on the Richter scale caused the Mississippi River to flow backwards.

173. In 1923, jockey Frank Hayes died while he was in a race but he still won. He suffered a heart attack while racing in Belmont Park in New York, but his body remained in the saddle until his horse crossed the line.

174. True fact: The Romans used urine to clean and whiten their teeth.

175. In 1927, Otto Rohwedder invented sliced bread. He patented the machine which sliced and wrapped the bread. Six years after getting the patent, more sliced than unsliced bread was sold. Hence, the origin of the phrase "the next best thing since sliced bread."

176. The child who was first delivered using anesthetic in 1847 was subsequently named Anesthesia. And yes, anesthesia is the next best thing since sliced bread, except that it came first before sliced bread – but yeah, you get the point.

177. The first policewoman was Alice Stebbins Wells. She joined the LAPD in 1910. Britain would have to wait another four years before it had its first policewoman.

178. Martin Luther King's real name was Michael King.

179. The Roman Empire, at its peak, covered an area of 2.51 million square miles. But wait, before you think that's impressive, consider that the Roman Empire was only the 19th largest empire in history.

180. The Roman Emperor Gaius once made his beloved horse a Roman senator. True fact.

All about Odd Locations and Addresses

In the Durango desert, in Mexico, there's a creepy spot called the "Zone of Silence." You can't pick up clear TV or radio signals. And locals say fireballs sometimes appear in the sky.

Image credit: www.blog.piktureplanet.com

181. What the picture said. Yes, that's creepy!

182. There is a city called Rome on every continent. True fact.

183. Underneath the streets of modern-day Paris is a network of tunnels known as the Parisian catacombs. The catacombs are a giant cemetery containing approximately 6 million bodies.

184. The driest place in the world is in Antarctica. Some locations in this remote continent do not receive precipitation of any form for several years.

185. The Mid-Atlantic Ridge is the longest mountain chain on earth estimated at around 40,000 kilometers. The ridge is a product

of the expansion of the Atlantic Ocean due to plate tectonics. Above ground, the Andes is the longest mountain range at about 7,000 kilometers in length.

186. The Dutch village of Giethoorn has no roads. Instead, the buildings in this quaint Dutch village are connected by footbridges and canals. Wouldn't it be fun if they had a sign at the village gate saying "Check your car here."?

187. The Haskell Free Library and Opera House is situated on the US-Canadian border. When used, the stage is in one country while half the audience is in another.

188. If you fancy a winter vacation, there's a resort in Finland were guests sleep in glass igloos so they can watch the Northern Lights.

189. Egypt is the world's oldest sovereign state. Let's just say the era of the pharaohs gave them plenty of a head start.

190. Saudi Arabia does not have any rivers within its territorial borders. None. Zero. Nada.

All about Astronomy and Space Exploration

Image credit: www.wtffunfact.com

191. Uranus' orbital axis is tilted at 90 degrees. The Earth's is tilted 23 degrees and this is responsible for the different seasons across the world. Venus is not tilted on its axis so it doesn't have any seasons.

192. The final resting-place of famed US Geological Survey astronomer Dr. Eugene Shoemaker is on the moon. His ashes were placed on board the Lunar Prospector spacecraft and crashed into a crater on the moon in 1996.

193. If you went out into space unprotected, you would explode first before you suffocate. The absence of air pressure means that your body exerts an outward force that is not counteracted resulting in a miniature explosion.

194. Buzz Aldrin is the first man to urinate on the moon shortly after stepping onto the lunar surface in 1969. Of course, he urinated into the urine bag in his space suit and not on to lunar soil.

195. Only one satellite has been ever been destroyed by a meteor: the European Space Agency's Olympus in 1993.

196. The first full moon to occur on the winter solstice, Dec. 22, commonly called the first day of winter, happened in 1999. When this happens, the moon appears about 14% larger due to the moon's closest approach to the Earth.

197. It takes 8 minutes for light from the sun to reach Earth. That means that the sun you see on the horizon is just a mirage. It was located there 8 minutes "ago" at the time that you see it.

198. Astronauts are not allowed to eat beans before they go into space. Passing gas in a space suit damages them.

199. Earth is the only planet not named after a god.

200. The biggest volcano in the solar system is located on Mars and it is called Olympus Mons. It is about three times as tall as Mt. Everest.

201. Powerful earthquakes can permanently shorten the length of the Earth's day. This can happen because strong earthquakes can disturb the Earth's spin. For example, the 2011 earthquake in Japan shortened our day by 1.8 microseconds while the 2004 Banda Aceh earthquake in Indonesia shortened the day by 6.8 microseconds.

202. Galileo Galilei is known for having invented the telescope but historians now believe that Johannes Lippershey, a Dutch eyeglass maker, may have beaten Galileo to it.

203. John Glenn is the first American to go into space. But he wasn't the first human to do it. Russian cosmonaut Yuri Gagarin was the first man in space.

204. Mercury is the closest planet to the sun but its dark side has can reach a temperature of -280F due to the absence of an atmosphere to trap all that heat.

205. The United States is bigger than Pluto. The longest distance in the contiguous United States is about 2,900 miles while best case estimates of Pluto's diameter puts it at about 1,400 miles. Take that Pluto!

206. In the solar system, Jupiter lays claim as the planet with the biggest ocean. The thing is, that ocean is made of liquid hydrogen and helium so you can just as well forget the idea of swimming in it.

207. One of Saturn's moons looks awfully similar to the Death Star in Star Wars. The moon's name is Mimas.

208. Ganymede, another of Saturn's moons, is the biggest moon in the solar system. It is even bigger than Mercury.

209. Hyperion, another of Saturn's moons, is so light that it will actually float in a tub of water (if there ever was a tub big enough to hold it.)

210. Speaking of floating on water, Saturn will float on water as well.

All about Science

Image credit: www.sosickwithit.com

211. The Amazon rainforest accounts for about 20% of the world's total oxygen production.

212. Hot water is heavier than cold water. This simple concept is responsible for much of the world's weather because the temperature differences allow water from the equator to move to the poles and vice versa. Without it, global weather would be significantly different.

213. Hot water freezes faster than cold water. This is formally known as the Mpemba effect.

214. Light doesn't necessarily travel at the speed of light. The speed of light refers to the speed at which light travels in a vacuum. The slowest we've ever recorded light moving at is 38 mph by a team of physicists led by Lene Hau of Harvard University.

215. Plutonium is the first man-made element.

216. The radioactive substance Americanium is used in many smoke detectors.

217. Sound travels 15 times faster through steel than through the air. Trackers who hunt using old school methods apply this concept by putting their ear close to the ground to listen for the vibrations generated by the movement of their prey.

218. A ball of glass will bounce higher than a ball of rubber. A ball of solid steel will bounce higher than one made entirely of glass. Making a ball of glass bounce, well that's something that we'll talk about another day.

219. Today, a chip of silicon a quarter-inch square, has the computing capacity equivalent to the original 1949 ENIAC computer, which occupied a city block. This progression in

computing capacity is best expressed by what is now known as Morse Law.

220. An ordinary TNT bomb relies on atomic reaction and should be called an atomic bomb. What we now call an A-bomb actually relies on nuclear reactions and should therefore be called a nuclear bomb.

221. Einstein's Theory of Relativity at work: if a jet plane travels at a speed of 1,000 kilometers per hour, its length will become one atom shorter than its original length.

222. When Anders Celsius developed the Celsius scale, he decided that freezing water should be set at 100 degrees and boiling at 0 degrees. The current system we know today was developed when his fellow scientists reversed the scale after his death.

223. A jiffy is an actual unit of time. It is official defined as $1/100^{th}$ of a second.

224. The line between two numbers when written in fractional form is known as the vinculum.

225. According to a study from the University of Northern Brittany in France, men are more attracted to women wearing the color red. This might not be science but who cares!

All about Technology

226. Ctrl+Shift+T restores your closed tabs in Chrome, and Ctrl+Alt+Shift+T restores entire closed windows.

227. Antibiotics are ineffective against viruses. They only work against bacterial infections.

228. Fill up your gas tank in the morning to get more gas for every dollar. Gas is denser in the morning due to the colder temperature so you get more mass per volume of gas pumped into your tank.

229. Every minute, we collectively send 200 million emails, generate almost 2 million Facebook likes, send 300 thousand tweets, and upload about 200 thousand photos to Facebook.

230. Google takes on about 3.5 billion search queries, in one day alone.

The first Computer mouse was invented by Doug Engelbart in around 1964 and was made of wood.

Image credit: www.thechive.com

231. The makers of Hewlett-Packard flipped a coin to determine whose name appears would appear first. The company also literally started right out of a garage.

232. The average computer user blinks at about half the normal rate when they are in-front of their computer.

233. The internet is growing very fast. As an example, about one million domain names are being registered every month. Good luck trying to view all those new websites.

234. In the US, about 12% of married couples first met online. Who says online dating doesn't work?

235. According to estimates, more people in the world own a phone than a toothbrush. About 4 billion people use a mobile phone while only about 3.5 billion use a toothbrush.

236. About 100 hours of video are uploaded to YouTube every minute. About 50% of them are about cute cats. Just kidding!

237. There are about 350 million Snapchat messages sent each day.

238. Douglas Engelbart invented the first mouse in 1963. It was made of wood.

239. About 97% of all emails sent everyday are spam.

240. 1 gigabyte is not equal to 1,000 megabytes. Instead, it is equal to 1,024 MB.

Miscellaneous Facts you Should Know

Dancing Goats

Legend has it...

Ethiopian shepherds first noticed the effects of caffeine when they saw their goats appearing to become frisky and "dance" after eating coffee berries.

Originally,
Coffee was eaten.

African tribes mixed coffee berries with fat which formed edible energy balls!

Image credit: www.mailments.com

241. Scary fact: on average, 12 newborn babies will be given to the wrong parents daily.

242. During the early days of printing when original print had to be set in individual letters, the capital letters were stored in the case on top while the lower case contained the small letters. This is why, today, we have "Upper Case" and "Lower Case" letters to refer to their original physical locations in the case.

243. True fact: Leonardo da Vinci could write with one hand and draw with the other at the same time. The man was plain brilliant.

244. Leonardo Da Vinci invented scissors, among other things.

245. The Guinness Book of Records holds the record for being the book most often stolen from public libraries. Perhaps it is too shiny and colorful?

246. If you have three quarters, four dimes, and four pennies, you have $1.19. You also have the largest amount of money in coins without being able to make change for a dollar.

247. Right handed people live, on average, nine years longer than left-handed people. On a related note, 2,500 left-handed people are killed per year from using products designed for right-handed people.

248. Frankenstein is the doctor, not the monster. The monster's name is, simply enough, "The Monster."

249. Sigmund Freud once advocated cocaine as a treatment for morphine addiction.

250. Old Coca-Cola actually included cocaine as an ingredient. True fact!

Conclusion

We hope that you enjoyed this short but informative book on all things fun facts! There are plenty more facts out there that we have yet to learn about and we should all take the time to try and learn something new every day.

Cheers.

Made in the USA
Middletown, DE
08 December 2015